SEVEN PRECIOUS CHARACTERS

ANANYAKUMAR MISHRA

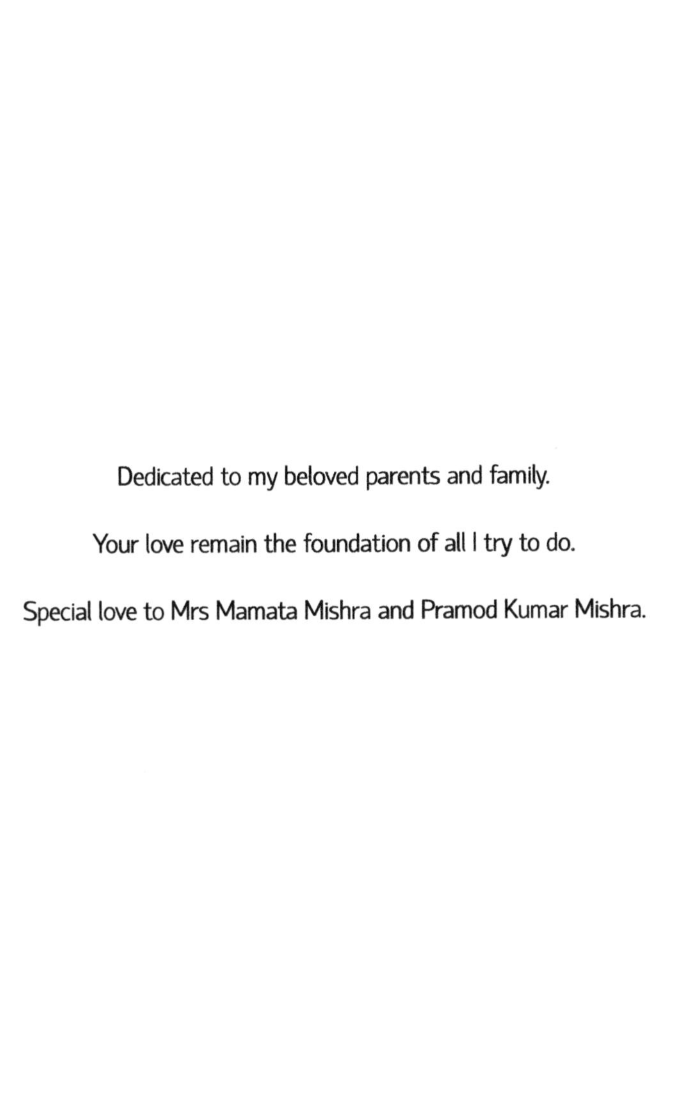

Dedicated to my beloved parents and family.

Your love remain the foundation of all I try to do.

Special love to Mrs Mamata Mishra and Pramod Kumar Mishra.

Contents

Preface

Thank you for choosing this book to read. This is just not a book but my dream. Labour of months, a result of those hours that I spent making, the time that took me away from my family and friends to a completely different world, my world of words and imagination. Life is a book in which you can't skip chapters. You have to read every line and meet every character. In this book, you will meet those seven precious characters of life whose existence can make a big difference. All the seven characters are important and have a specific value and role in our life, and the most magical power of these seven characters is that you can pick any of the characters to get the essence of the other six.

I pour my heart and soul into this book. I know what it feels like to lose myself in the words on the page. With each new chapter, each new page, I found a new challenge. I know the fact that each one of us is aware of these seven characters but somehow in the journey of life, we forget to value these crucial parts of our life. My motive behind writing this book is to remind me and my readers the value of these gems.

CHAPTER ONE

GOD- THE SUPER POWER

A power that is beyond our knowledge, experience, consciousness, logic and understanding, the shape of whom can't be measured in any physical quantities, the gender of whom can't be decoded by any great biologist, the picture of whom can't be taken by any powerful camera, the name of whom can't be given by mere humans is someone the most powerful creature, a supernatural power, a great architect, a great engineer, a great mathematician, a great poet, a great musician, a great warrior, greatest in almost all the fields, he is the creator of himself and the creator of what we see, what we feel, what we touch, what we taste, what we smell and also the creator of whatever we are inventing in the physical world. He is the Lord of time and also the destroyer of time. He is beyond time and space, the reason for existence and also the reason for the smooth functioning of the world. He created believers and also non-believers, theists also atheists, good also bad, dharma also adharma, God also Devil, man also a woman. I believe in an essence that extends beyond the physicality of the matter or energy universe and even though I can not quantify its being, its presence is real. Perhaps this is a function of my individuality, but as much as I have tried to shrug off its presence and succumb to scientific materialism, I simply cannot. All power I believe ultimately resides with the superhuman which can not be fully articulated, reduced or even truly conceptualized, however, its presence is ubiquitous. I envision the superpower of God as multifaceted and this is a consequence of omnipotence. It can be perceived on many levels. The powerful God that is 'the transcendence' from which our soul originates from that personal God is the one that I communicate with. The laws of physics do not limit the superpower as all its constraints and realities are ultimately a product of the same superpower. He is consequently the cause of why something, as opposed to nothing, exists. In Hindu Upanishads, it is written- "That supreme Brahman is infinite, and this conditioned Brahman is infinite. The infinite proceeds from the infinite. If you subtract the infinite from the infinite, the infinite remains alone." He is a thought that keeps you calm, listens to everything you have got to say and has the power to solve all your problems, also he is the positive energy that fills you with confidence, inspiration and balances all your negative emotions.

Let us think about human civilization. We, humans, are relatively new to this playground Earth. Dinosaurs and other extinct species came and enjoyed a lot before us. The earth itself is somewhat new to this game, in this still massive playground, the universe. Some scientific theories stated that the Earth and its ocean somewhat crystallized from the molten mess and space dust that was the early solar system. Orbiting the one star we should hold responsible for our evolution. The sun formed from the nebulae which were pumped with elements from the remnants of an ancient star that went into supernovae. Dying, so that things such as carbon, and oxygen can make our molecules and fancy stuff like Gold and silver can adorn or jewellery. The sun and the solar system are located in one of the arms of a galaxy we call, The Milky Way. The sun is but an insignificant speck compared to our Galaxy. The Milky Way contains about 200 to 400 billion stars and about 100 billion planets. Here we are unaware until the invention of the telescope, that we belong to something so massive. Even We used to believe Sun is revolving around us. Let us look further, and even the enormous Milky Way becomes a speck compared to the gargantuan size of the Universe. There are about a hundred billion galaxies in the observable universe. Can you imagine it?

There are 100 billion galaxies,
One particular Milky Way has 400 billion stars,
We orbit one such star out of the 400 billion.

The universe has existed for 13,700,000,000 years and Humans have existed for only about 2,00,000 years. That's about 0.0014% only. Do you still consider yourself significant in this huge cosmos? Do you still believe your ideologies are practical and correct? Do you still believe your science and technology can defeat the superpower and can prove him void? Do you think a normal sound human can process all that mind-boggling existential nihilistic information without thinking of some coping mechanism? Yes, He exists! He exists everywhere in every form. It requires special eye power to see Him, a special ear to listen to Him and Purest mind to feel Him. God is a verb, not a noun. If God were a person, place or thing, He would be an alien. God is not an alien being. He is BEING.

Finite views of humans about infinite God invariably err. He is not comparable with anyone else. He need not fit into our concepts about love, justice, fairness etc. because He alone is the ultimate reference for all the above qualities. Except He, everything else is delusion and temporary. Sometimes I believe Him as in an entity, an entity that controls how we conduct our lives. Mind you, not the basic pattern of life we lead, but its intricacies, such as those little choices you make every day. I respect this God, and believe that it may be benign or not depending on your perspective. Because the God I am describing now is my conscience.

The only hope that comes to our mind during the worst situation of life is the hope of God. God can not be circumscribed by human language since that would render Him limited to human possibilities. God is not a being like human beings are. God is not a being among beings. He is the foundation of all beings, and outside of Him, nothing exists. We create an image of God and sometimes we call those images Gods. But they can't be the ultimate superpower, the supreme being. God can't be drawn on small paper or made with mere clay.

Do you find yourself questioning God's existence when you are faced with difficult situations? Are you often frustrated with negativities in life? Is it hard for you to trust God with the challenges of life? People have different perceptions of the picture of God. Some see Him as Ram or Krishna, some others as a vengeful dictator. Many people fear God because they have a distorted understanding of His character. God not only want you to view him correctly but also wants you to feel Him intimately. Your self-image will improve once you realize the awesome greatness of God and the works He places on you. The more accurate your understanding of who God really is and how he is involved in your life, the more highly motivated you will become to excel in the use of your precious time, talent and abilities. He is loving, merciful and faithful, and he never betrays. God is completely trustworthy. Allow the truth about Him and all His marvellous character to transform you.

If you want to understand the importance of God in human life, go to the desert and ask a thirsty person, how he feels after getting a glass of water? Let me tell you a story of my graduation time. I was a student from a Physics background. One of my juniors asked me, "do you believe in God and can you prove it with the help of Physics?" At that time I was silent and start thinking about it. Finally, I got the solution from my inner soul. I answered him like this, Think about the microscopic organisms. Can you see them? No, you can't. But they can be viewed under a high power microscope. They are living creatures residing their life in only one dimension of Earth's coordinate system. They can not able to see us as our size is so huge as compared to them. Hope you understand what I meant to say. They can not see us as their size is too small compared to us, even though they do not have any idea about the existence of human life or any other creatures in this universe. Do we exist or not? Yes, we do. Do they know? No. Can you say this, because they don't know, we do not exist. You can not accept it ever. This is the concept I want to tell you, as because you can not able to see Him, you say He is not there. Maybe he is not the creature from a three-dimensional coordinate system. He is the creature of even a more complicated coordinate system to which normal human brain can't reach.

You may have listened from people that man created God in his own image. Ancient man, when they didn't understand what caused an eclipse, plague, and most naturally occurring cataclysmic events needed some ways to explain them. When they ventured out at night, many were taken by predators but soon realized, that if they went out only when the sun was out far fewer died, bringing about the worship of the first God, the sun. Things only went downhill from there, groups of like-minded people began grouping and start believing that their way of worshiping their particular beliefs of Gods was the only thing that could protect them from all negativities and devils, the first religions were formed. Gradually with the emergence of new ideologies and beliefs, with the result of loopholes of the previous, new religions and beliefs to different Gods formed. I am not at all biased on a particular religion or God, my belief is only for the supreme being who is beyond all. I personally believe that God is not something we can explain using modern science and technology or language. No amount of experiments and words that one can use to truly describe the complexity of who or what God is and what (s)he or it can or can't do. Where (s)he or it presents, how (s)he or it came to be, etc. If someone or something is able to describe God, it would simply be incomprehensible to our feeble minds to fathom. This is one of the reasons people argue about it so much. Because everyone has their own version of the truth and I find it very unlikely that anyone exactly knows the true nature of God.

CHAPTER TWO

MOTHER- THE CREATOR

I begin with the broad statement that every human being is the result of procreative experience. This procreative experience and resulting birth action transpire via a mother. Mother is a divine female who creates a new creation and helps in the continuation of life processes in this universe. She is the one taking the topmost position in this beautiful creation. With widespread roles in this earth, sometimes she becomes the biological mother responsible for the creation, sometimes a surrogate mother responsible for giving birth to the child of another woman, and also she takes diverse forms like stepmother, a putative mother or adoptive mother etc. In the context of mother, let me remind you of the great mothers like Yashoda, Bachue, Parvati, Venus, Kwan Yin, Queen Maya, sita, Rani Laxmibai etc. Historically, the roles of the woman was confined to being a mother or wife and taking care of its family by living in home. But, this perspective is changing gradually with the awareness in female education, female-centric policies, and the self-dependant mentality of females. Now they are the first teacher of a child. Throughout history mothers with their children are seen in different artistic works, such as painting, sculptures, or writings. At the end of the nineteenth century, Mary Cassatt was a famous painter known for her portraits of mothers. A mother is the only person in the world with whom our soul gets connected before coming to this physical world. The invisible bond between her and you is much stronger than the ionic bond. The lap of a mother is the first educational institution for every child. It is the first temple, she is the foremost God, she is the maker of home, the nation, the universe. Our ancient culture believes that on the woman depends, the sustenance of the whole country. That is why the country is referred to as the motherland.

"The hand that rocks the cradle is the hand that rules the world" is a poem by William Ross Wallace that praises motherhood as the preeminent force for change in the world. A mother is the toughest warrior, having strength stitched with strings of softness, love, and care. Mothers are unmatched, exceptional, someone who sees the best in their kids even when they drive her crazy, the doppelganger of superman - one who can make all missing things appear at once. One ideal that binds us all in the society beyond the limitations of time, space, beyond any bounds of geographical and cultural practices, or of time and age is the ideal of the all glorified mother. The simple, yet perpetual truth that we all have our mother who creates, nurtures, and protects is the common thread that binds the society. It is also the perceptible string that binds humanity to divinity. The divine Mother, Devi Adi parashakti, manifests herself in various forms, representing the universal force- both creative and destructive. She becomes the mother nature to give birth to all the life forms as plants or animals and sustain and nourish through her body. Ultimately she reabsorbs all life forms back into herself or devours them to sustain herself as the power of death.

The most silent, the most painful, and the most resilient battle one can ever fight is the one fought by the mother, yet goes unnoticed, for she can accommodate the whole universe in her womb. The restless nine months, the sleepless nights, the vomiting and the blotted tummy and the imperfect body - it takes a lot of guts and courage to be a mother. A tummy with ugly stretched marks is indeed a body with tigers stripes, the symbol of bravery. Be it a cesarean or a normal delivery, a mother endures through all the pain proving she could weather the strong. How delicate yet strong the womb is! It is not a mere organ, all with flesh and blood but like a sword tearing every hardship apart to hold on to an entire life to come up. How fragile yet fierce the opening is, capable of pushing a new beginning out of a tiny hole.

When they pick their child up, they can feel the map of their bones beneath their palms, or smell the scent of their skin embedded in their child's skin. This is the most extraordinary thing about motherhood, finding a piece of herself separated yet connected, something a mother can not live without. The bond between a mother and a child is stronger than a hurricane. How angelic the bond is that a mother understands the very inaudible voice of her child. She knows exactly the time when her child feels a little hungry, she understands the fear of her newborn child. The bonding develops in the brain of a mother before the birth of her child, you may have listened sometimes when a child feels something inside the womb, he or she kicks, and the mother feels that. How great that mother who creates, nourishes, cares till her last breath. That beautiful hug relaxes the most complicated stress, and that lovely kiss cures the most convoluted anxiety. She is the only one whom you can trust blindly and with whom you feel the ultimate security.

A mother is perceived to bear one of the most important roles in our lives. A mother's role starts from being pregnant and maintaining a human life for long nine months and eventually giving birth to the child with the risk of losing her life.

She is the best teacher who starts teaching you so many things knowingly or unknowingly after your birth. You just need to follow her hectic unpaid work schedule to learn the most important lessons of human life like time management and responsibility. Sometimes I think how all mothers can able to manage things so perfectly without doing any specialization in MBA? Without having any psychology master's degree she is the only person who knows you best, your feeling, your emotions, your needs, your worries, your interest, and so many other things that I don't need to elaborate I guess. She also becomes the nurse during the crying of a baby or the stressful situations of adults. She also monitors what her child would eat, and change her diapers during small age. Her voice is more than medicines, it can heal the painful wound in a short duration, she does these things also without having any medicinal degrees. I guess she should be awarded the topmost degree in hotel management. Because it is also a fact that can not be denied by anyone, she is the best chef in the world, not even the food of five-star hotels can replace the delicious taste of her food. One can easily learn the financial matter from her mother because she plays the role of financial controller in a family. She is a person with diverse skills and the person who stand out the most in all situations from birth to death. She is an incarnation of the

Goddess having multitasking talent. To think of describing mother in words is like counting stars in the sky.

"They questioned, what exceptional can mothers do?

The universe replied, they bleed and breed what none can do!!"

Though many people influence values in your life, I believe there is one person who showed you a lot more than the rest and this lovely lady is no other than your mother. She taught you to strive for whatever it is that you want, she makes you believe that you can achieve anything you want if you work hard because she is the only person who possesses a hundred percent confidence in your hard work without even knowing much about the position you want to get in your life.

She is the most valuable person, a symbol of love, compassion, patience, vision, inspiration, and determination. Mother is not only just a word but the basis of living. Without a mother, there is no life that we can expect in this world. "Maa" is the first word for all of us, which we remember in every sorrow and pain before the name of God. She is the only person who spent most of her time with you, she wants to discuss every event that happened with you in school or with your friends. You may have seen sometimes while you discuss something with your father, without even knowing what you are discussing, she will be there in the kitchen listening to your words. She is the only person on the planet whose eyes are filled with tears before you. You may have seen that sometimes your father scolds you for something and you cry, she also cries with you, because she can't control her emotions when you become depressed. She gives you company during your studies, games, eating, drinking, bathing, and so on.

When teenage hits, your mind becomes your first enemy which instructs you to get involved in valueless things. At that time you can not understand your mother's emotions well. Maybe due to puberty your mind gets attracted towards girls or boys, I mean to say about the time of yours when opposite genders get attracted towards each other. she wants you to focus on studies, but you do not listen to her much. But my dear, no one can be a better guide than your mother. Never scold her for these silly reasons and follow her blindly to reach your goal. You can share your feelings during this complex time period of teenage with your mother. Trust me, you will never fall prey to negativities. Maa... You are the best creation, you are my creator, you are amazing, and no one can replace you and your face from my mind. Love you a lot.

A mother is only a mother, no matter whether she is opulent or penniless, no matter whether she lives in a palace or a shed. No amount of success, money or fame can give the satisfaction and warmth, a mother could. The strength of a mother is second to none. Even when she is in times of stress, when she is fighting her over demons, when she is beyond exhausted nothing stops her from gathering strength altogether to remain tranquil and keeping her motherhood at the very forefront, no matter what, the audacity and aura of a mother are unmatchable, equivalent to the divine being. We as a child always take our mother for granted because she remains available for us at every moment. But it's my heartily request to all that try to understand her emotions and try to make yourself available for her in all situations. Life is really worthless without her. She is a precious gift by God that we need to keep with utmost love and care.

To honour motherhood, maternal bonds, and the influence of mothers in society, Mother's Day is celebrated on different days in many parts of the world, most commonly in the month of March or May. In India, it is usually celebrated on the second Sunday of May. In Hindu tradition, Mother's Day is called " Mata Tirtha Aunshi" or "Mother Pilgrimage fortnight", and is celebrated in countries with a Hindu population, especially in Nepal, where mothers are honoured with special food. The holiday is observed on the new moon day in the month of Vaisakha. In Buddhism, the festival of Ullambana is derived from the story of Maudgalyayana and his mother. In Islam, there is no such concept as Mother's Day, but the Quoran teaches that children should give priority to loving their mother over their father. You will find so many different religions, so many different countries celebrating their Mother's Day in different ways.

Let me share with you a fictional story from my childhood, which was once told to me by my grandma to motivate me,

I wrote that idea in one story named " A Miracle".

Life loses its charm when melancholy wraps over its shiny beautiful surface. After long trouble, it was able to rise up! Really it is an examination conducted by almighty for a living being. God always helps and supports humans. He gives opportunities after opportunities, but many can't take it due to some ordinary reasons, they run behind short-lived pleasure, possessions, and temptations and knowingly forgive long-lived eternal pleasure. I would like to describe a truth but unbelievable, honest but doubtful, real but surprising, emotional but heartbreaking, a tragic but miraculous story of my sweet mythological grandmother.

Those were the days when tradition touches the apex, corruptions, lies, cheating, violence, etc. were the microscopic minorities that mingle over pure noble ideologies. All have big faith in God. Wow! What a beautiful life. She believes in God as a maniac and worships Him from the core of her heart and is totally dedicated to omnipresent. In those days, maintaining five sons and a drunkard husband was a herculean task. Her husband was an eminent teacher of that locality. He wasted more than half of his salary on drinking. It was really difficult for a lady at that time to maintain five sons with a little amount of money. She is a God indeed, who optimizes her courage level to infinity and can provide all sorts of noble ideas, possessions, and basic needs.

A most reminding tragedy occurred in her life when her four sons were affected by pox. She had no rice to cook for her family. She was having no idea. With full of dedication toward God, she just cried a lot. After a few minutes, she entered her worshiping room and became astonished by seeing an ant house full of rice. She thanked God with a balmy mood. She remembered that every day she used to give rice to ants, that rice by multiplying thousand times came to help her during her needs. It's the grace of God.

CHAPTER THREE

FATHER- THE NOURISHER

Many male animals of the animal kingdom do not participate in the nourishment of their young child. The evolutionary development of humankind as creatures and the involvement of offspring's upbringing took place during the stone age. In Medieval and most of European history, caring for children was predominantly the work of mothers, whereas fathers in many societies provide for the family as a whole. Since the 1950s, social scientists and feminists have increasingly challenged gender roles, including that of the breadwinner. Policies started targeting fatherhood as a tool for changing gender relations. Research from various societies suggests that since the middle of the 20th-century fathers have become increasingly involved in the nourishment of their children.

A father is the tallest pillar of a family. Fathers are pivotal in a child's life. Fathers are of different kinds and their relationships with their children. However, they form one of the crucial influences in a child's life, along with mothers. Daughters are provided with a sense of security by their protective fathers, and sons model their attitudes toward their toiling fathers. Fathers are an essential part of a family's support system. Along with mothers, they teach us important values and skills. They not only influence who we are within but how we have relationships with people as we grow. The way a father treats his child will influence what he looks for in other people. Friends, lovers & spouses will all be chosen based on how the child perceived the meaning of a relationship with his or her father. The pattern a father sets in the relationships with his children relates to other people. They have an impact on relationships that children make as they grow and help make us become who we are today.

One of the most crucial influences a father can have on his child is indirect, father influences their children in large part through the quality of their relationship with the mother of their children. A father who has a beautiful relationship with the mother of their children is more likely to be involved and spend time with their children and to have children which are emotionally and psychologically healthier. In the above context, I knew it from my father during my childhood only. My father used to ask me a question before going to bed during my childhood, which is "whom do you love most or who do you give first priority in your priority list?" It put me in a dilemma because both were there on the bed, one on my left side and the other on my right side, my inner sense wanted me to say both, but papa told me to choose one. After five minutes of thinking, I asked whom do I choose? His answer was so simple -"Mother".

Papa... You are truly amazing. A father never denies buying you a toy or a bar of chocolate during your childhood, if you have a strong obsession with that particular object or food. He knows, you will break the toy after a few days, but he will buy it for you because you will not cry after getting that. You must come across some situations where your father disapproves of some of your needs. You might get angry or frustrated during that time. My request to you is that please never be the same frustrated again. Because if I tell you the fact you will get emotional, Sometimes your father will not tell you about the financial worries, the burden of his office. Instead of all problems, he comes forward to just fulfil your desires. He never considers your desire worthless, sometimes it is! He works hard and hard not to live a comfortable life or to wear branded clothes, nor even to eat in a five-star restaurant or to go for a trip, but you know whenever you point your finger at anything, he buys anyhow for you. Never give much pressure on your father. Let me share with you the view of DR. Michel Lamb about the image of low-income urban fathers as disengaged and less involved with their children.

"Our research bashes the stereotype of the low-income father. These fathers care about their kids, but may not show their love and affection in conventional ways and sometimes a lack of a job, poor communication with the mom, or even their own childhood experience can prevent them from getting involved."

Too often, we may assume that a low-income, urban dad who does not live with his children is not involved with, even not concerned about, his children. This can push a father away from his family. My request to all of you is that we should aware of this fact and support our fathers during their emotional needs. We should be very comfortable with our father and try to figure out the unspoken stress inside him. Sometimes that stress may lead to high blood pressure or brain stroke. We should not let our papas struggle alone, we should be there by their side like they always do.

How can one forget the best experiences with a father from the very beginning of life? By touching his little finger, a baby starts to know about the surrounding, he teaches to say maa, papa, dadi, dada and many more, also he teaches about different things and living beings of the surrounding, a baby forgets many a time, but without getting frustrated a little, he says again patiently. He is the one whose hugs relaxes the mind, he is the same one whose scary stories like "Bara neka tera kaan" makes you sleep. A person with the highest number of degrees in all fields is none other than that papa. He may not have university-affiliated degrees, but at that time he is the only person who makes you dream about getting the highest degree. Seating in front of the scooter, hands below the hands of papa on accelerator and travelling and enjoying the natural beauty and feel like riding alone, or sitting in the train or aeroplane for the first time with him, one-on-one conversation about current affairs, playing almost all games, by holding his hand going to school and that happiness and excitement in horseback riding were the amazing experiences you might have got.

He never looked for praises, never one to boast, he just works harder and harder to make your life beautiful. Truth be told, whatever I am writing today or contemplating ideas is only due to the lessons taught by my father. He is the one who taught me to understand, to read, to write and to express on a white paper. You are my inspiration papa. Love you a lot.

Anyone can father a child, but being a papa takes a lifetime. Everyone would describe their fathers differently. They all have different equations and experiences. A father and his child may not always speak but understand each other well, They do have a silent conversation with their child. They do understand the unspoken frustration of children, but they do not speak all the time because they want us to learn how to fight in the toughest situation in the future. Like Lord Krishna Of Mahabharata, he becomes the charioteer of our life's chariot till his last breath. Words can not describe his greatness.

The bond of a father and a child is so invisible, it's an imaginary force that can't be viewed under naked eyes nor even by the high powered microscope. It's beyond the range of science and technology too. A father becomes the first companion of a child just after its birth and trusts me he is the best companion who will stand with you in the worst situation of your life. He is the first friend and the last love of your life. He is the one who dared to place the world's hopes and dreams in our hands.

Many studies do suggest that daughters look for a man who may be similar to how their father was with them; if he was nurturing or strong. Sons see their fathers as role models, whom they should grow up to be like and imitate their behaviour.

father has always supported me to chase after my dreams and pursue what interests me, knowing the risks. He believes that everyone must make mistakes to learn from them. Fathers are known to be risk-takers in this way. They help to instil problem-solving abilities so that we can do better.

Since time immemorial, there have been many stereotypes about how fathers are the breadwinners, and mothers must take care of the house. In the evolving age of feminism, mothers are now working and pursuing careers, while fathers are trying to help take care of the household. A modern father should always support his spouse's career and he always appreciates the balance that they create between work and home. He helps her with chores and even makes sure to have food on the table when she is busy with work. A father teaches that family is essential, and no matter what, family is always there for one.

While some fathers may seem strict and disciplined, it is because they want their children to learn how to deal with the real world. Fathers have an essential role to play when it comes to their children, forming

relationships, as they are influenced by how their father treats the family. A good father doesn't discern between his children and always respects his wife, as mothers, too, are an important part of the emotional well-being of a child. Children still want to make their mothers proud.

They seek emotional and physical comfort from their fathers in tough times and look to them for enforcing rules.

Fathers also help build a child's self-esteem. A father helps the child to be proud of whom he is and stand up for what he believes. He teaches benediction, perseverance and being true to oneself. A father takes up all kinds of responsibilities, from providing for the family to making sure that their children are safe. Father is a person who lets you experiment with life in your way and pulls you up when you fall. He is with you always, especially when you need him. We can't be in this world without our fathers. No matter how successful we are, our first identity is that of someone's son or daughter. Salute to all Papas!

Often, fathers feel the burden of their responsibilities but are conditioned not to show it. That sometimes interferes with both their ability to express affection and our ability to recognize it.

Fathers don't always enjoy the glow of intimacy and admiration we give our mothers. Indeed, fathers have the cultural image of breadwinners, disciplinarians, authority figure. We often did hear our mothers say, "just wait until your father gets home!" or, "don't let your father know about this!". Traditionally, our culture has often put fathers into a very difficult role. They must be aloof but intimate; must earn the wage, but be present; must be compassionate, but disciplinarian.

There is another context that I want to write here is about Non-human fatherhood. I come to know about these things from some biological journals. It is all about Non-human fatherhood. You will be astonished to know, Most of the waterfowls like geese, swans, gulls, loons, and a few species are most protective for their child during travelling, they usually travel in a line and the father is usually the ones guarding the babies at the end of the line while mother leads the way. Also, the female seahorse(hippocampus) deposits eggs into the pouch on the male's abdomen. The male releases sperm into the pouch, fertilizing the eggs. The embryos develop within the male's pouch, nourished by their yolk sacs. Fathers in a few primate species care for their young. Those that do are tamarins and marmosets. Particularly strong care is also shown by siamangs where fathers carry their infants after the second year. In titi and owl monkeys fathers carry their infants 90% of the time with "titi monkey infants developing a preference for their fathers over their mothers." Many more examples are also there.

The idea of a special day to celebrate and honour fatherhood was first introduced in the United States. It is celebrated on the third Sunday of June every year for that special person in our lives who we call father, remember that he may seem remote but likely is more close to you than you realize. He may be the definition of "tough love," but it is love. Even if one's dad, father or "old man" is grumpy, opinionated and distant, remember that more likely than not you are more important to him than one can imagine. So, it is our responsibility as children, and as spouses to return his affection by respecting and loving him. In any case, embarrass dad with an abundance of attention, praise and even small bits of acknowledgement, because this begets one of the most priceless expressions from a father;

Fathers are the most important part of this creation without whom this universe is impossible. It is to thank our fathers for what they do for us every day. Love your father, every day...

CHAPTER FOUR

GURU- THE GUIDING STAR

Teachers hold the key to securing our future. They are invisible hands that mould and shape society. They are pillars of the nation-building process because they help to influence the next generation to become moral, responsible, and productive members of our community. Their daily work in the classroom will impact the well being of the economy and the success of society. Teachers are the front-line worker of the education system and play a major part in shaping the values, knowledge and skills of the students. They impact students at a time when they are most susceptible to influence and equip the students so that they can grow up to fulfil their dreams, passion, and goals. And bring out the potential of students and ignite their worth and contributions. Some of the students will also become key leaders of the community. Teachers are gatekeepers, opening doors to opportunities and possibilities that are beyond the foreseeable horizon. They trigger visions, develop building blocks, and catalyze actions to build the world to come. They are crucibles that forge the strength, achievements, and growth of society. Teachers are major equalizers in life. They help to transfer knowledge and skills and model the right conduct so that students can learn and have equal opportunities to succeed. They help students to develop multiple pathways to achieve their dreams. Teachers are builders of human lives and architects of the future. Their contributions ensure the survival and sustainability of our world. They are co-authors in crafting life stories and the history of humanity.

There is enough evidence available in our Holy Scriptures; Shrimad Bhagwad Geeta and Vedas that whenever there is a dearth of virtues and a decline in faith in God, then God either himself descends or sends his messenger to restore the lost virtues with the help of true spiritual knowledge.

In Yajurveda Chapter 19 mantra 25-26 that a true enlightened saint or a True Guru will have true spiritual knowledge and will impart the way in three parts.

Another identity of a true enlightened saint or a True Guru is that he will accept charity (guru dakshina) only from his disciples, not from any other person. This fact is also verified by the verse from Yajurveda Chapter 19 mantra 30.

Another way to identify a True enlightened saint or True Guru is that he will impart the way of worship in three stages. This fact is verified by Shrimad Bhagwad Geeta chapter 17 verse 23 and Sankhya number 822 Samved Utarchik Adhyay 3 Khand no. 5 Shlok no. 8.

Shrimad Bhagavad Gita chapter 4 verse 34 talks about obtaining this way of worship from a Tatvdarshi (enlightened saint) or True Guru who has complete spiritual knowledge. And in chapter 15 verses 1 to 4, the identity of a True Guru has been given.

In Shrimad Bhagavad Gita 15 verses 1 to 4, 16 and 17 way of identification of a True Guru (Tattavdarshi or enlighted saint) is given. It is written that a True Guru would be the one who can differentiate all the elements of the upside-down eternal tree of the universe, whose roots is the Supreme God.

The greatest Guru, is the One, within you. He has been with you, is with you and will be with you, irrespective of what you do, whether you acknowledge His presence or not, without any judgement and is ever ready to guide you, to show you the light to find Him. His love and compassion for you are unconditional and the purest form of love. You can call Him Shiva, God, Allah, Jesus, Buddha, Guru Nanak or any other name. He is the same, He is the Supreme Consciousnesses. He who becomes wind in the wind. It means if you call your guru out of the air/wind/water/ or from the rays of the sun or anything, if he possesses the capabilities to come on your call, it means he is a true guru. There are three levels of guru.

First is Manavaug guru:- one who teaches people about what to do and what not to do. They show you the path of dharma to the common man. They would teach you about scriptures. They do mainly Satsang.

Second is Divyaug guru:- one who teaches you about sadhana, yoga, tantra, mantra, astrology etc to the common man. They don't believe in teaching instead they give you sadhanas that will teach you.

The third is Siddhaug guru:- These are those who teach the divyaug guru. These are not accessible to the common man. They are commonly Siddhas and reside mainly in siddhashram. These are mayabi and you can't recognise them as long as they don't reveal themselves or you haven't reached a very high level of consciousness.

And then come those who are called Mahaguru or satguru. Although I have written only about three types, but there is one more category. Since it is very rare, they don't need to be classified. These are the guru who is the most knowledgeable and the most powerful, they can teach you anything. Whatever vidyas or sadhanas you guys think has got extinct, they still have that and can teach you that. They are shiv themselves. One more speciality is that these gurus can be accessed even after their death. You can only access your teacher as long as he resides in his body, the moment he leaves it, you are left with nothing. These are the gurus that make krishna 'krishna' and Ram 'Ram'. They have no existence of their own, they have submerged themselves in Shiv in such a way that there is only shiv and not him.

There is a fundamental difference between a teacher and a guru. A teacher is the one who teaches us about the objects and processes of the external world, while a guru teaches us the techniques of exploring the reality of our inner being. To understand the difference between gurus and teachers, I explored a lot and found beautiful writings. I am attaching one of that herewith

Difference between a Guru and a Teacher!!!!!!!

1. A teacher takes responsibility for your growth.

A Guru makes you responsible for your growth.

2. A teacher gives you things you do not have and require.

A Guru takes away things you have and do not require.

3. A teacher answers your questions.

A Guru questions your answers.

4. A teacher requires obedience and discipline from the pupil.

A Guru requires trust and humility from the pupil.

5. A teacher clothes you and prepares you for the outer journey.

A Guru strips you and prepares you for the inner journey.

6. A teacher is a guide on the path.

A Guru is a pointer to the way.

7. A teacher sends you on the road to success.

A Guru sends you on the road to freedom.

8. A teacher explains the world and its nature to you.

A Guru explains yourself and your nature to you.

9. A teacher gives you the knowledge and boosts your ego.

A Guru takes away your knowledge and punctures your ego.

10. A teacher instructs you.

A Guru constructs you.

11. A teacher sharpens your mind.

A Guru opens your mind.

12. A teacher reaches your mind.

A Guru touches your spirit.

13. A teacher instructs you on how to solve problems.

A Guru shows you how to resolve issues.

14. A teacher is a systematic thinker.

A Guru is a lateral thinker.

15. One can always find a teacher.

But a Guru has to find and accept you.

16. A teacher leads you by the hand.

A Guru leads you by example.

17. When a teacher finishes with you, you celebrate.

A When a Guru finishes with you, life celebrates.

Let us honour both, the teachers and the Guru in our lives...

Hope you find the difference I am trying to explain. If one can buy wisdom, there will be no importance of true knowledge. Anyone could excel in life. Google is more multi-talented, multi-skilled than us, it answers most of our real-life problems and bookish stuff. So google should be our topmost priority and best guru of life. But it is not so. We don't possess that respect towards google or any other digital platform answering our queries. This implies Guru does not only teach or explain, he/she makes us feel the reality and the truth of our existence. He is the guiding star guiding millions to reach their milestones. Remember, meeting a true Guru is the highest achievement of one's life. Meeting Him will change your way of thinking, your understanding of life forever.

Every other day some of the other big 'guru' gets exposed and it is natural to think where should one put in his/her faith with the least chance of getting cheated in the name of spirituality. I have written so many things about a true Guru. Now let me write about who should not be considered as a bonfire guru.

Never fall for a guru who gives you a mantra that can be found in any of the spiritual books. The point is, no mantra is written anywhere in any book whatsoever. What is written is simply a prayer or a verse/shlok. If anyone is giving you something like that calling it a mantra, it simply means that this so-called 'guru' doesn't know anything himself.

Do not believe anyone who tells you that a revered figure like Shiv or some deceased saint can be your Guru. A Guru should always be alive and accessible. If you can not access your Guru easily or can not talk to him freely then there is absolutely no point in having a Guru.

Stay away from the gurus who talk about kundalini initiation. If anyone talks about the word ' kundalini', be sure he knows nothing. Anyone who promises self-realisation or enlightenment or kundalini awakening for a price is genuinely fake.

Stay away from a guru who initiates you in any manner or gives you a mantra online or through a video link or in the presence of other people. Initiation is a secret. If anyone gives a mass initiation, then be sure he is simply faking it, he doesn't know anything himself.

Always stay away from a 'guru' who initiates you the moment you approach him. Any genuine Guru will take his own sweet time which may run into years, testing you on various grounds before giving you the simplest practices forget about initiating you immediately.

Never ever get trapped in this word called dhyan/ meditation. All we hear these days is meditation, this or that type. This meditation is the biggest scam of this century. People say that it is written in so many scriptures that one can realise or can reach God through meditation. True, it is written but the point is nowhere in any old scripture it is written that how to do meditation. Neither any realised soul be it Shiv, Ram, Krishn, Buddh ever told anyone how to do it. What we see in the name of meditation these days are the tricks created by individuals out of their own minds. They have nothing to do with meditation. Meditation happens at a very high state of mind and it can not be induced by any action whatsoever. It is the most guarded secret of ancient lineages and no matter how much money you pay, you can never learn it unless you spend years and years in the company of true Saints and Gurus. What is being sold in the name of meditation is simply a trick to keep one's mind occupied for a few minutes while it keeps dreaming about meditation.

Never fall for any 'guru' who says that do this kriya or mudra after paying me so much and you'll realise God. If anyone uses these words, simply do not fall for him. All these kriyas and mudras have been created by fake gurus who wanted a larger spiritual empire and for that, they needed some easy tricks which anyone can do and which can be sold on a mass basis. You may keep practising them for your whole life but they won't take you anywhere.

One should never go to a guru whose 'technique' one can easily buy through his various franchise outlets. One must understand that God neither comes so cheap nor is He so easily available at one's nearest outlet.

Do not fall for a popular and commercial guru. Anyone who has a corporate-like structure wherein you can simply pay and learn tricks devised by him from his so-called volunteers is a fake guru. One is most likely to fall for these fake gurus in our time and that is because you buy what you see. These so-called realised gurus spend millions of dollars on their advertisements on social media and through their PR firms. Now when one keeps seeing them selling tickets to realisation whenever one switches on his/her cell phone or laptop, one obviously gets impressed. But what one doesn't realise is, it is all created this way so that one gets impressed and buys their ticket to realisation. It all is nothing but a marketing gimmick.

India is known for so many eminent true gurus. To honour the importance of gurus in India, we celebrate Guru Purnima in the month of Ashadha (July-Aug). The word "Guru" in Sanskrit is translated as "dispeller of darkness." A Guru dispels the seeker's ignorance, allowing him to experience the source of creation within. The day of Guru Purnima is traditionally the time when seekers offer the Guru their gratitude and receive his blessings.

CHAPTER FIVE

FRIEND- THE MOTIVATOR

One would believe that the larger the company is, in which we are engaged, the greater variety of thoughts and subjects would be started in discussion; but instead of this, we find that conversation is never so much straightened and constricted as in numerous assemblies. When large numbers of people meet together upon any subject of discussion, their debates are taken up mainly with forms and general positions; no, if we come into a more contracted assembly of men and women, the talk generally runs upon the cricket, fashion, news and the like public topics. In proportion as the conversation gets into clubs and knots of friends, it descends into particulars, and grows more free and communicative; but the most open, interactive discourse is that which passes between two persons who are familiar and very close friends. Friendship is the invisible bond between two or more persons that not only helps each other to motivate during the worst time but also helps in healing dreadful wounds. A friend is the one who accepts and loves the imperfect, flawed and messed up you. They are the ones who will run to you even if you call them in the middle of the night.

They love and accept you for who you are. You can share your darkest and deepest secrets with them without the fear of being judged. They stand with you through sunshine and storm, through thick and thin. They motivate you to become a better version of yourself and help you to face your fears. A true friend is the one who stays with you beyond any distance, time or words.

Humans have been termed ultra-social animals because our lives tend to be extensively socially intertwined and our psychological and physical health is powerfully influenced by our relationships. Abundant evidence indicates that psychological and physical well-being is strongly related to social connections, as seen in perceived social support, integration in a social network, marital quality, and the quality of close friendships. A person may connect with many persons in their life. However, the closest ones become our friends. You may have a large friend circle in school or university, but you know you can only count on one or two people with whom you share everything and hence true friendship. There are essentially two types of friends, one is good friends the other is true friends or best friends. They're the ones with whom we have a special bond of love and affection. In other words, having a true friend makes our lives easier and full of happiness. Above all, true friendship stands for a relationship free of any judgments. In a true friendship, a person can be themselves completely without the fear of being judged. It makes you feel loved and accepted. This kind of freedom is what every human strives to have in their lives. In short, true friendship is what gives us reason to stay strong in life. Having a loving family and all is okay but you also need true friendship to be completely happy. Some people don't even have families but they have friends who're like their family only. Thus, we see that having true friends means a lot to everyone. Friendship is important in life because it teaches us a great deal about life. We learn so many lessons from friendship that we won't find anywhere else. You learn to love someone other than your family. You know how to be yourself in front of friends. Friendship never leaves us in bad times. You learn how to understand people and trust others. Your real friends will always motivate you and cheer for you. They will take you on the right path and save you from any evil. Similarly, friendship also teaches you a lot about loyalty. It helps us to become loyal and get loyalty in return. There is no greater feeling in the world than having a friend who is loyal to you. Moreover, friendship makes us stronger. It tests us and helps us grow. For instance, we see how we fight with our friends yet come back together after setting aside our differences. This is what makes us strong and teaches us patience. Therefore, there is no doubt that best friends help us in our difficulties and bad times of life. They always try to save us from our dangers as well as offer timely advice. True friends are the best assets of our life because they share our sorrow, soothe our pain and make us feel happy.

Now, Let's understand the various types of friendships. Aristotle described three types of friendships (or *philia* [1]): utility, pleasure, and virtue friendships.

Utility friendships are best understood as having the primary purpose of making it possible for individuals to obtain valued outcomes for themselves through exchanges with others. Therefore, the primary value of utility friendships is the degree to which relationships serve as a means to each friend's desired ends. A friend might have particularly helpful skills, relatively greater popularity, or physical strength. Because the relationship is based on a history of conferring benefits on one another, if that utility falters, so does the relationship. Friendships based on utility mirror the common idea that the point of friendship is to provide benefits for the friends, a view that has been enshrined in social exchange and interdependence theories of relationships (Huston & Burgess, 1979; Van Lange & Rusbult, 2012).

The second friendship type, pleasure friendships, has the primary purpose of providing enjoyment or pleasure. As long as the friends continue to obtain this pleasure, they will remain friends. This form of friendship mirrors the contemporary focus of psychological research on how friendship contributes to satisfaction and positive emotions. For example, one study showed that for older adults, friends are important because they are associated with short-term pleasurable feelings resulting from spending time together playing sports, engaging in hobbies, or attending cultural activities.

Aristotle (1999) viewed the third type, virtue friendship, as the best form of friendship because the individuals in these relationships are beneficial and pleasurable, but the relationship is defined by three distinctive features. First, the individuals are friends because they admire one another's good qualities. The good qualities (virtues such as honesty, sympathy, generosity, fairness, and courage) of the friend are what attract and bind the friends together. Because good qualities can be assumed to be a stable pattern of acting and being, these friendships are expected to last longer. Second, virtue friends see the friendship and their shared activities and goals as valuable in themselves. This is distinct from pleasure and utility friendships, wherein the primary goal of the interactions is to obtain outcomes such as enjoyment and received help. Finally, Aristotle suggested that virtue friends want the best for one another, for the friend's sake. This means that obtaining benefits and experiencing pleasure for oneself are secondary to the value of one's friend and of the friendship itself. Virtue friends benefit one another, but they do so spontaneously to enhance the friends' welfare, without keeping track of or equalizing benefits. The non-accounting aspect of virtue friendship has some similarities to the concept of communal relationships, but Aristotle differs in emphasizing the importance of the good qualities of each friend. The emphasis on the characteristics of friends is important because those good qualities make it possible to have the best kind of friendship.

Friendship improves happiness and abates misery, by doubling of joy and dividing of grief. I shall beg to leave to quote some out of a very ancient author, whose book would be regarded by our modern wits as one of the most shining tracts of morality that is extant if it appeared under the name of Confucius, or of any celebrated Grecian philosopher; I mean the little apocryphal treatise entitled the wisdom of the son of Sirach. How finely has he described the art of making friends by an obliging and affable behaviour; and laid down that precept, which a late excellent author has delivered as his own, that we should have many well-wishers, but few friends? "Sweet language will multiply friends, and a fair speaking tongue will increase kind greetings. Be in peace with many, nevertheless have but one counsellor of a thousand." With what prudence does he caution us in the choice of our friends! And with what strokes of nature, I could almost say of humour, has he described the behaviour of a treacherous and self-interested friend! " If thou wouldest get a friend, prove him first, and be not hasty to credit him; for some man is a friend for his own occasion, and will not abide in the day of thy trouble. And there is a friend who, being turned to enmity and strife, will discover the approach." Again "Some friend is a companion at the table, and will not continue in the day of thy affliction: but in thy prosperity he will be as thyself, and will be bold over thy servants. If thou be brought low he will be against thee, and hide himself from thy face." What can be more strong and pointed than this following verse? "Separate thyself from thine enemies, and take head of thy friends." In the next words he particularizes one of those fruits of friendships "A faithful friend is strong defence; and he that has found such as one has found a treasure. Nothing does countervail a faithful friend, and his excellency is invaluable. A faithful friend is the medicine of life; and they that fear the lord shall find him. Whose fears the Lord shall direct his friendship aright; for as he is, so shall his neighbour, that is his friend, be also."

Let me share with you some ideas that I learned from Wikipedia and some other resources regarding Friendship at different ages of human life. The actual meaning of friendship in children tends to be more heavily focused on areas such as common activities, physical proximity, and shared expectations. These friendships provide opportunities for playing and practising self-regulation. Most children tend to describe friendship in terms of things like sharing, and children are more likely to share with someone they consider to be a friend. As children mature, they become less individualized and are more aware of others. They gain the ability to empathize with their friends and enjoy playing in groups. They also experience peer rejection as they move through the middle childhood years. Establishing good friendships at a young age helps a child to be better acclimated to society later on in their life. Based on the reports of teachers and mothers, 75% of preschool children had at least one friend. This figure rose to 78% through the fifth grade, as measured by co-nomination as friends, and 55% had a mutual best friend. About 15% of children were found to be chronically friendless, reporting periods without mutual friends for at least six months.

In adolescence, friendships become "more giving, sharing, frank, supportive, and spontaneous." Adolescents tend to seek out peers who can provide such qualities in a reciprocal relationship, and avoid peers whose problematic behaviour suggests they may not be able to satisfy these needs. Personal characteristics and dispositions are also features sought by adolescents, when choosing whom to begin a friendship with. Relationships begin to maintain a focus on shared values, loyalty, and common interests, rather than physical concerns like proximity and access to play things that more characterize childhood. A study performed at the University of Texas at Austin examined over 9,000 American adolescents to determine how their engagement in problematic behavior (such as stealing, fighting, and truancy) was related to their friendships. Findings indicated that adolescents were less likely to engage in problem behavior when their friends did well in school, participated in school activities, avoided drinking, and had good mental health. The opposite was found regarding adolescents who did engage in problematic behavior. Whether adolescents were influenced by their friends to engage in problem behavior depended on how much they were exposed to those friends, and whether they and their friendship groups "fit in" at school.

Friendship in adulthood provides companionship, affection, as well as emotional support, and contributes positively to mental well-being and improved physical health. Adults may find it particularly difficult to maintain meaningful friendships in the workplace. "The workplace can crackle with competition, so people learn to hide vulnerabilities and quirks from colleagues. Work friendships often take on a transactional feel; it is difficult to say where networking ends and real friendship begins." Most adults value the financial security of their jobs more than friendship with coworkers.The majority of adults have an average of two close friends.Numerous studies with adults suggest that friendships and other supportive relationships do enhance self-esteem.

Friendships are never constant. People change with time. Only one or two would remain by your side as friends in the long run. Most friendships will lose sheen to eventually end over a period of time. Never let those people go who stuck by you through the thin and thick of life. We meet people. We become friends with them, sometimes close friends. Then life happens and we change locations. We become busy with our new lives and lose contact. Close friends soon become casual acquaintances, even strangers. Life in the present world is extremely fast. People keep moving from one place to the other due to easy mobility options. Gone are the days when people used to stay in the same place forever. As a result, most friendships don’t last long. We might promise each other that we would always stay in touch and always be close friends. We might even make a conscious effort to be in touch for a few months. But then those daily messages soon turn to a message per week, a message per month, and finally maybe a casual "Do you remember me? We used to be friends in school" after many years. But then such is life. It moves on.

Friendship Day is celebrated on the first Sunday of August in India. On this day, we honour the bonds of friendship we form through the course of our lives that enrich us and make us happier. Friends might not be our family, but they bring equal amounts of happiness in our lives, share the same amount of love and stick by us, no matter what. And this day is all about making them feel special. This day was first proposed in Paraguay in 1958 as International Friendship Day. However, it is believed that it first originated from Hallmark cards in the 1930s, whose founder was Joyce Hall. Friendship Day started as a marketing strategy at first. Hall designated the day to celebrate the people closest to us, who matter the most, and in the process, send them a card to show them that we're thinking about them. The marketing strategy shaped an official holiday, announced by the US Congress in 1935, to be celebrated on the first Sunday of August every year.

CHAPTER SIX

LOVE- THE SAVIOR

Maybe that was the joyous day when I saw a lovely face with captivating eyes and honey-sweet lips, lilac soft, sculpted figure, which was twin thin, the waist was tapered and had a burnished complexion, a pair of the arched eyebrow on sweeping eyelashes, her delicate ears framed a bottom nose, dazzling angle-white teeth gleamed as she blew gently on her carmine finger-nails, really it was very pleasurable to see her flowing, moon-shadow black hair, enticing, constellation-black eyes gazed at somewhere in a white paper, really she was having a bouncy personality and a sugarcane voice, want to listen again and again, want to see her vibrant clothes again and again. Maybe that was a special day when my heart beats want to increase and interested to change its function of pumping blood to feel the sacred love, by indicating breeze to flow gently from her with a lovely fragrance, eyes want to communicate with her jolly eyes but there was no green signal from her. Sometimes it happens, when you start feeling day as night and night as day by forgetting the time fleeting, ha... ha... what a romantic madness! Her beauty captures me but what amazes me is that it is wonderfully combined with her amazing soul, I wonder how I could not notice such a magnificent flower like her before, even if she does not believe that she is beautiful. I often say look into my eyes and you will be surprised by your pretty reflection. I remember the poem of Lord Byron whenever I imagined that beautiful angel-

" She walks in beauty, like the night
Of cloudless climes and starry skies;
And all that best of dark and bright
Meet in her aspect and her eyes;
Thus mellowed to that tender light
Which heaven to gaudy days denies.
One shade the more, one ray the less,
Had half impaired the nameless grace
Which waves in every raven tree,
Or softly lightens over her face;
Where thought serenely sweet express,
How pure how dear their dwelling place.
And on that cheek, and over that brow,
So soft, so calm, yet eloquent,
The smiles that win, the tints that glow,
But tell of days in goodness spent,
A mind at peace with all below,
A heart whose love is innocent!

In the above poem, Lord Byron focuses on female beauty and explores the idea that physical appearance depends upon inner goodness and if in harmony, can result in the romantic idea of aesthetic perfection. One can easily understand the idea of true love from the above poem.

Oh, my heart stops beating faster........... I said to my inner soul and even argued with him but he did not listen to my single word. Just like a Panic attack, I feel a sudden episode of intense fear or anxiety. After a fraction of seconds of the above situation, dopamine starts flowing slowly slowly........ I touched my hands, went to the mirror, look at myself again and again by thinking as if I am dreaming again...My soul told me in a low pitched voice "your conversation of two days was about 1245600 seconds and that's real" I sat silently with my white paper to pen down a few words that I wanted to say from a long day. Yes, I feel a unique vibe all the time I saw your face. This is not my today's emotions, it began from years. It's not just infatuation or bodily attraction but a true eternal encounter of my soul and mind, it's the purest true waves from my heart that no one can see. Let me quote something, words of Epicurus, " *satis magnum alter alteri theatrum sumus ";* as if man, made for the contemplation of heaven and all noble objects, should do nothing but kneel before a little idol, and make himself a subject, though not of the mouth, yet of the eye; which was given him for higher purposes. It is a strange thing to note the excess of this passion, and how it braves the nature and value of things, by this; that the speaking in a perpetual hyperbole is comely in nothing but in love. You are the best creation I have ever met, frankly speaking, God might have recruited special engineers in heaven to create you. I know you might have got so many proposals on this day or some other days in the past, for me, the past is a waste paper and I don't want to propose you as they did. I want my soul to connect with your soul and say whatever I want to say. I want a silent conversation between both the souls. The day my soul listens to your soul's feelings, I will be the one saying "I love you" first.

Beyond the horizon of reality and fiction, rights and wrongs, there lies a region, the region where all my conscience, all my logic fails, where all my presumption deceives, the region where I forget all my agony and ecstasy, tragedies and fortunes, achievement and failures. The region where I am entirely lost in your eyes, forgetting everything else. I will be waiting for you there, not forever, but till my last thought reminds you, till my last emotions forget you, beyond which I will have no more control over my life. Beyond this, I will have to fulfil the expectation of my people, the ones who nurtured me, the ones whom I owe a lot.

You may be thinking now that I have written the above romantic lines by thinking about someone special in my life. But it is not so. It is just a romantic description of an imaginary girl to make you understand how the love of couples in this world can be portrayed. In my perspective, Love is something beyond the above writings, it is sublime power that binds the whole universe in a single thread. It's a powerful invisible emotion that saves the world from all negativities. It is the best pain killer, which can heal the wounds of bullets. In some cases, it is a romantic powerful emotion, and in some other cases, it's a revolutionary tragedy. Sometimes it helps, sometimes it destroys. In love, you lose yourself. You forget who you are. The only world you live in is theirs. Love is like a psychedelic drug, we think a lot before we start but once we started, we can't let it go. The beep sound of her notification or the unique ringtone you saved for her is more powerful than the strong sound of the alarm. Love is the best feeling that anyone feels in the universe. And when you feel it, you understand no limits. There is no difference between falling in love and being in love. It's not like falling off a cliff, which is terrifying because you know you will eventually hit the ground and probably die. Falling in love is like falling into something that has no floor. It is great and exhilarating and a bit scary, but mostly great, and when you feel it, you should allow yourself to enjoy it. You talk about things you'll do together in the future without realizing you are talking about the future. When you say, "I miss you," it's because you really do miss her after only a day apart. It's not only just a cute thing to say, it's a real ache that says she is a part of your life.

Let us now try to analyse whether all lovers we see in the universe are doing love or they just feel infatuation with each other. There is a small line between love and attraction. Most of the time we say love to mere attractions. Those tickling sensations in the stomach, that burning sensation in the heart, that funny feeling, that wide smile may not be love but the result of a strong attraction. It might fade sooner or later. In love you are happy most of the time but not being loved back might make you feel sad sometimes but in attraction, one just craves for just one's happiness rather than thinking about the other person. Love is not always " we are together forever, " it may be only shown in movies. Some people are not meant to be together but always in love, love can be felt but in attraction, you make each other feel loved even if it doesn't exist. Attraction is like "you are mine, I am yours" while love is like "we are one." Insecurities can only be there in case of attraction but when you love someone truly, you might feel jealous sometimes, but at the end of the day you're just" one", no one can end that love even if you are not together. Love never brings along that feeling of guilt, fear, anger, frustration or anxiety but attraction brings all these negativities. Love stays somewhere deep inside even if the person you love lives far away from you, but in attraction, the relationship can end in seconds.

Lord Krishna also gave a beautiful explanation regarding love and attraction in Mahabharat. According to Him, love comes from compassion, while attraction comes from ego. Love says- May my children get all success, glory, pleasures of the world, attraction says- I will give my children all the success, glory and pleasure of the world. Love says- I am proud of my children, no matter if he is successful or not, I wish him all the very best in life. Attraction says- The world should be proud of my children and his accomplishments and he is the best son/daughter, the world has ever seen. Love gives liberation, while attraction gives attachment. Love is Dharma, while attraction is Adharma.

Barbara Fredrickson, a leading researcher at the University of North Carolina at Chapel Hill, presents scientific evidence to argue that love is not what we think it is. It is not a long-lasting, continually present emotion that sustains a marriage; it is not the yearning and passion that characterizes young love, and it is not the blood-tie of kinship. Rather, it is what she calls a "micro-moment of positivity resonance." She means that love is a connection, characterised by a flood of positive emotions, which you share with another person- any other person- whom you happen to connect within the course of your day. You can experience this micro-moment with your romantic partner, child, or close friend. But you can also fall in love, however momentarily, with less likely candidates, like a stranger on the street, a colleague at work, or an attendant at the grocery store.

Love is a divine emotion that connects two souls. Real love is hard to find. Love doesn't happen in couples only, it starts before one's birth, the unconditional love of the mother when a child is present inside the womb is the first and truest form of love one can find before coming to this world. After mom, one finds love from a father, family, friends, teachers, relatives, pets, and many more. The degree of intensity of love may be different among different individuals but, the only constant force that helps to bind everyone is love. Ancient Greek philosophers identified six forms of love: essentially, familial love (in Greek, *Storge*), friendly love or platonic love (*Philia*), romantic love (*Eros*), self-love (*Philautia*), guest love (*Xenia*), and divine love (*Agape*). Modern authors have distinguished further varieties of love: unrequited love, empty love, companionate love, consummate love, infatuated love, self-love, and courtly love. Numerous cultures have also distinguished *Ren, Yuanfen, Mamihlapinatapai, Cafuné, Kama, Bhakti, Mettā, Ishq, Chesed, Amore, Charity, Saudade* (and other variants or symbioses of these states), as culturally unique words, definitions, or expressions of love in regards to a specified "moments" currently lacking in the English language.

Psychology depicts love as a cognitive and social phenomenon. Psychologist Robert Sternberg formulated a triangular theory of love and argued that love has three different components: intimacy, commitment, and passion. Intimacy is a form in which two people share confidences and various details of their personal lives and is usually shown in friendships and romantic love affairs. Commitment, on the other hand, is the expectation that the relationship is permanent. The last form of love is sexual attraction and passion. Passionate love is shown in infatuation as well as romantic love. All forms of love are viewed as varying combinations of these three components. Non-love does not include any of these components. Liking only includes intimacy. Infatuated love only includes passion. Empty love only includes commitment. Romantic love includes both intimacy and passion. Companionate love includes intimacy and commitment. Fatuous love includes passion and commitment. Lastly, consummate love includes all three components. American psychologist Zick Rubin sought to define *love* by psychometrics in the 1970s. His work states that three factors constitute love: attachment, caring, and intimacy.

Following developments in electrical theories such as Coulomb's law, which showed that positive and negative charges attract, analogues in human life were developed, such as "opposites attract". Over the last century, research on the nature of human mating has generally found this not to be true when it comes to character and personality—people tend to like people similar to themselves. However, in a few unusual and specific domains, such as immune systems, it seems that humans prefer others who are unlike themselves (e.g., with an orthogonal immune system), since this will lead to a baby that has the best of both worlds. In recent years, various human bonding theories have been developed, described in terms of attachments, ties, bonds, and affinities. Some Western authorities dis-aggregate into two main components, the altruistic and the narcissistic. This view is represented in the works of Scott Peck, whose work in the field of applied psychology explored the definitions of love and evil. Peck maintains that love is a combination of the "concern for the spiritual growth of another," and simple narcissism. In combination, love is an *activity*, not simply a feeling.

Psychologist Erich Fromm maintained in his book *The Art of Loving* that love is not merely a feeling but is also action, and that in fact, the "feeling" of love is superficial in comparison to one's commitment to love via a series of loving actions over time. In this sense, Fromm held that love is ultimately not a feeling at all, but rather is a commitment to, and adherence to, loving actions towards another, oneself, or many others, over a sustained duration. Fromm also described love as a conscious choice that in its early stages might originate as an involuntary feeling, but which then later no longer depends on those feelings, but rather depends only on conscious commitment.

CHAPTER SEVEN

DEVIL- THE DESTROYER

You will be surprised to know that the word devil and the word divine have the same root. Both the words come from the Sanskrit root "Deva". The word "deva" means divine. Without God, the devil can not exist. With God, all devils disappeared. There must be a balance in the universe. If you believe in good, you must believe in evil. If you don't believe in one, how can you define the other? How would you know light without darkness, happiness without sorrow, positive charge without negative charge or sweet without sour. The devil and God are the two sides of the same coin. If there is God, there is a devil. If there is no God, there is no devil. They come together and go together. We are either awake or asleep, being awake from inside can be the metaphor for God, or being asleep internally can be the metaphor for the devil. Whenever we think about the devil, we think of an ugly person or animal with flesh as red as blood has horns coming out of his head and has more than two hands, more than one head. Precisely we assume an abnormal body shape with a negative and furious personality. Some think of a doll that doesn't only look scary but also can move from one place to other and can harm people. Shadows in the dark can also be represented as the devil in "light out." There are different names of the devil i.e, Lucifer, Beelzebub, Moloch, satan, ghost, lord of files, Ravana, Kansa, and many more. All the devils seen on the TV screen or in books are having different negative qualities like pride, greed, lust, envy, gluttony, wrath, sloth, etc. There is just the objectification of a hostile, destructive and negative force. They relinquish untruths and try to distract the believers from God.

We create a thought or We are forced to create a thought about a negative force or what We say, the devil. From that thought, we write scary books, create horror movies, and justify their existence. If we want to argue about the existence of the devil based on our thought processed by a small brain, our arguments might be baseless. Our mind is not capable enough to understand the existence or understand the different creatures of the universe. When I was a child, I had a very furious image of the devil. I still remember, the big bald head with bare hair on it, poke-marked big flat face, big red eyes popped out of the socket, big nose, abnormal lips, mouth wide opened, with fire coming out continually from the mouth. His neck connected with a thin green pipe with the body. He had more than ten hands with different deadly weapons on them. He was so tall and huge, maybe more than a hundred kg weight. Ha... ha... I don't know, why this type of creativity used to come to my mind. I used to enjoy scary stories during my school time too. All had different furious experiences as if all had seen the devil in real life. You might be laughing at this writing. But the truth is that society creates a very negative and furious personality as the devil to control the mind of the human race by making them threatened.

European people during the 1200s believed that there were dragons, and these dragons could fly and could breathe fire. This belief came about because dinosaurs' bones were found in farmer's fields, etc. Those people also did not know what lightning was? They put two and two together and came up with flying dragons, whose fire breathe could set their thatched roof on fire. Ideas such as these, because of lack of scientific knowledge about things we take for granted now, made sense to them. If there were anything they are afraid of it was the fire. They had no idea to put it out and did not even know, why their houses were catching fire(In reality their houses were catching fire due to heavy lightning). Superstitions like this continued and soon fire was involved in hell, persons committing sins had to go to hell and for purification, they had to burn themselves on hot water or fire. Scientifically, there is no devil, no hell. The devil is simply the leftover remnant of fear and superstitions that unfortunately there inside them. Religions take advantage of this devil to scare people, believing it will make people act "better". It is also a convenient excuse for why things go wrong because no one wants to blame God for wrong things. The existence or creation of the devil is only to criticize him. The idea of foisting a devil on people or making people believe their bad luck or disease is the work of the devil is sadistic and immoral

Let's understand the power of demons, devils, and genies from the ideas of some notable classical scientists. They used to believe these negative powers could be helpful in the process of evolution, working of computers and certain experiments. For them, these strange beasts are not a creature of superstition and pseudoscience. According to the physicist James Clerk Maxwell, a demon can reverse entropy. The seventeenth-century French philosopher Rene Descartes conceived of the disturbing possibility that some devious spirit could hijack our sense of reality. This 'malicious demon' would affect what we think we see, hear, smell, and touch. French mathematician Pierre-Simon Laplace proposed that some demonic intellect would be able to calculate the past and future of anything if it knew the precise location and trajectory of all particles and all forces acted on it. Maxwell's tiny demon operates a door between the compartment in a gas-filled vessel, choosing when to allow molecules to pass from one side to the other. His demon also demonstrates the surprises that can arise from probability theory, because every once in a while, the rarest of rare events would occur, such as only the fastest gas molecule passing through that hole. Canal's Bohm's demon also helps in the survey of thought experiments on the uncertainty in quantum mechanics. Searle's demon, named after the US philosopher John Searle, is a powerful nanobot(also known as a nanoscale demon) that could control which neurons in a person's brain get stimulated and which do not. There were also descriptions of some quantum level demons by Marie Curie. Whatever research or ideas scientists during that classical time gave were rejected during the modern time, and modern scientists believe the idea of the devil is baseless and stupidity.

If there were no evidence in favour of devils, why there is a notion of that negative force in the universe? There must be certain existence of the devil in some invisible form, maybe the real devil presents in all human bodies in different forms. They are the enemies, they are the real devils. They bind the soul in the life cycle and are confined in this material world with illusion. The most powerful devils present inside all of us are as follows,

1) Kama (desire or lust)
2) Krodha(anger)
3) Lobha(greed)
4) Mada(arrogance)
5) Moha(delusion or infatuation)
6) Matsyara(jealousy)

Let's understand each context elaborately for a better understanding.

1) Desire or Lust- In Hindu, Buddhist and Jain literature, Kama means desire, wish, longing, the pleasure of the senses. All creatures just after their birth come to feel a desire, desire is also of two forms, one is positive and the other is negative. When the desire is positive, it is the aesthetic enjoyment of life, it's divine love, affection. But when it becomes negative, it is converted into lust and becomes the reason for the erotic personality of human beings. Persons having erotic personalities live in a distressing situation. For them, life is all about sex and they believe to capture everything through it. They act, feel, and think in certain different ways which can be reflected in their behaviour. They live in the world of sensual and sexual experiences, infused with fancies and wishes often to satisfy the unfulfilled sexual and sensual urges, longing and unresolved conflicts.

"Lust is a psychological force producing an intense desire for an object, or circumstances while already having a significance of other or amount of the desired object. Lust can take any form such as lust for sexuality(libido), money or power. It can take such mundane forms as the lust for food(gluttony) as distinct from the need for food. It is similar to but distinguished from passion, in that passion propels individual to achieve benevolent goals while lust does not."

In the Bhagavad Gita, Lord Krishna declared in chapter 16, verse no. 21 that lust is one of the gates to Narka or hell.

Arjuna asked- O descendant of Vishnu, by what is one impelled to sinful acts, even unwillingly, as if engaged by force?

Krishna replied- It is lust only, Arjuna, which is born of contact with the material mode of passion and later transformed into wrath, and which the all-devouring sinful enemy of the world. As fire is covered by smoke, as a mirror is covered by dust, or as the embryo is covered by the womb, the living entity is similarly covered by different degrees of this lust. Through them, lust covers the real knowledge of the living entity and bewilders him. Therefore O Arjuna, the best of the Bharatas, in the very beginning curbs this great symbol of sin by regulating the senses and slaying this destroyer of knowledge and self-realization. The working senses are superior to dull matter; the mind is higher than the senses; intelligence is still higher than the mind, and even the soul is higher than the intelligence. Thus knowing oneself to be transcendental to the material senses, mind and intelligence. O mighty-armed Arjuna, one should steady the mind by deliberate spiritual intelligence and thus by spiritual strength conquer this insatiable enemy known as lust.

2) Anger- Krodha means anger, which is a result of not getting what you desire. When one becomes angry, he wants to destroy, to harm, to break, to fight. He forgets reality and doesn't pay attention to what is right and what is wrong, wants to win only. After becoming angry one becomes more aggressive towards life, reacts violently to injustice, may fight with others unnecessarily, be assertive or sometimes may react too harshly. It is proven medically

that the long term effect of anger leads to high blood pressure, anxiety, headache, heart disease, peptic ulcer, stroke, diabetes etc. Hence, anger does not only affects the external relationship but also affects mental health and damages the body. Anger is not the solution to any problem, it may be the creator of more complicated problems. So be calm and if you are feeling like you can't able to control your anger, go to the nearest medical for treatment.

3) Lobha(greed)- It is also a great enemy of humans. You might be aware of a fact of all, humans always need something more than what he had. For example, during childhood, when you had no bicycle, you wanted to buy a bicycle for going to school or for showing up to your friends. Once you pass that childhood age, you start contemplating for a stylish bike to show up or to ride without pedalling. Meaning you don't want to put effort into pedalling, rather you want the comfort of riding a racing bike and reaching your destination faster. When this desire of your fulfilled, you start contemplating a luxurious car because now you don't want dust to touch you or sunlight to reach you. You want more comfort and this goes on. This is the result of an in-build instinct present in every human. Those able to kill this greed become the happiest. The result of greed is an acquisitive personality where a person becomes more self-centred. Kindness, compassion, benevolence, and charity like positive traits that are not found in them. They are never satisfied with what they have and possess a strong desire for more and more wealth and power. So keeping a check on greed is very important to lead a hassle-free and cheerful life.

4) Arrogance- Arrogance is a behaviour or feeling that one displays to show up his superiority over others. Let

me explain it more clearly. You can be very correct for whatever fact or opinion you want to express, but people just don't like to listen to you. Most probable this is because of arrogance. In opposite, you can be wrong and naive in your communication, but people around you just like to listen to you. Even if the message is wrong and illogical, they may find it funny and enjoyable. People will also come around and give you good advice if you are wrong and if you have a good attitude. Arrogance will come back and hit you. You are restricting your opportunities and the growth of any relationship you have by being arrogant. Even if someone is wrong, you don't have to point it out bluntly. Be easy and nice to your peer group; be respectful to people more senior and elder than you. Arrogance is a naive attitude that causes ignorance and hatred. It is detrimental to all dimensions of life. Arrogance is a quality easily exhibited by people who think they are smart. Indeed, they are not even smart enough to realize that it is probably the worst way to present smartness.

5) Delusion or Infatuation- Infatuation or Moha is a state of mind where the mind doesn't want to understand reality. It creates its ideologies and beliefs for a person or situation and saves it in memory and tries to puzzle the human mind. It is a very negative devil which closes the eyes with an invisible blindfold. Impractical hope and imagining things in a different form are the results of infatuation. An infatuated person lives in a state of hypnotism. They have strong feelings of liking and disliking and their state of mind changes at regular intervals. These persons may have strong attachments with persons or things. Some medical researchers state it is a symptom of a mental disorder.

6) Jealousy- It is a feeling or showing an envious resentment of someone on their achievements, possessions, or perceived advantages. Jealousy arises in the human mind mainly due to less self-confidence, poor self-image, fear or insecurities. If you understand your inner value perfectly, you will never become jealous, and if you are still jealous then that is the devil destroying you. Lord Krishna in Bhagavat Gita Chapter 12 and verse 15 has said "one who does not envy but is a compassionate friend to all, such a devotee is very dear to me." Aristotle defined "envy as pain as the sight of another's good fortune, stirred by those who above what ought to have." Bertrand Russell said that envy was one of the most potent causes of unhappiness. Not only is the envious person rendered unhappy by their envy, Russell argued, but that person may also wish to inflict misfortune on others to reduce their status.

We try to find the devil in the external world but it is present inside everyone. It is not harmful nor even fearful if you can control it, if you love to live with it, it can be the reason for your complete destruction. These all devils are interconnected with each other. Referring again to the holy Bhagavad Gita, chapter 2 verse 62 -

" While contemplating the objects of the senses, a person develops attachment for them, and from such attachment, lust develops, and from lust, anger arises."

and chapter 2 verse 63-

"Anger leads to clouding of judgement, which results in bewilderment of memory. When memory is bewildered, the intellect gets destroyed; and when the intellect is destroyed, one is ruined."

Here in the above two verses Lord Krishna clearly explains the devils of Arjuna which were stopping him to start fighting. Now in this present world, we don't need to fight against others but to fight against our inner negativities to lead a blissful life.

9 798886 670080

Printed by Libri Plureos GmbH in Hamburg,
Germany